© Celeste Doaks

Cornrows and Cornfields

© *All copyrights remain with the author*

First Edition

ISBN 9871903110218

Cover Design by
Owen Benwell

Published in 2015 by

Wrecking Ball Press
Danish Buildings 44-46 High Street, Hull HU1 1PS. England

Cornrows and Cornfields

celeste doaks

Wrecking Ball Press

Acknowledgements

I'd like to thank the following publications for printing the first versions of the following poems:

"The First Time I Heard the F Word" - *Spillway Magazine*

"Dropped Brown Egg" - *Asheville Poetry Review*

"Black Lotus" - *Obsidian: Literature in the African Diaspora*

"God Bless the Mothers" - *Obsidian: Literature in the African Diaspora*

"No Leftovers" Connotation Press, an Online Artifact connotationpress.com/a-poetry-congeries-with-john-hoppenthaler/2011/april-2011/814-celeste-doaks-poetry

"Lunch Time at Holy Cross" - *San Pedro River Review*

"Father-Daughter Time" - *Bayou Magazine*

"Note to Don Cornelius" - *Tidal Basin Magazine*

"My Last Day at Holy Cross" - *Home is Where, An Anthology of African American Poets from the Carolinas*

"Joan's Grace" - *Fledgling Press 14*

"Joan's Grace II" – *Fledgling Press 14*

"Dad's Golf, A Foreign Language to Me" *Chicago Quarterly Review*

"memory before body" *Chicago Quarterly Review*

"Single Twin Band Crush" – Split This Rock Poetry Database www.splitthisrock.org/poetry-database/poem/single-twin-band-crush

Thanks

Now for the crucial part. Crafting poetry, like making any art, requires a village of supporters. Therefore, let me begin naming my pillars. Grandma Lillie Kyle, you continue to be my guiding light. I want to thank my parents: John and Myrtle Doaks. They are the reason the rumble began. Without their consistent encouragement and support, this flower would've withered a long time ago. Next up is my brother Cedric. He's my hood heartbeat that has my back in every city and foreign country without question. To my nephews, CJ and Cameron, from the day you were born you filled my heart. An extra special thanks goes to my primary poetry mentors, Dorianne Laux, Joe Millar and Patricia Smith. Patricia your eyes were the first to see this manuscript and your guidance was priceless.
(I know you're already raising a glass of white wine!) To my poetry parents, D and Joe, you'll forever be the calm who sheltered me literally and physically in the City of Oaks. And of course, I could not forget Momma Sonia Sanchez. Thank God those priceless words of wisdom you shared on our train ride back to NYC years ago, never left my cerebrum. This title is a tribute to your literary love and resistance.

In addition to the people who kept my dream alive, I owe thanks to the institutions and organizations where the actual work began. All the dedicated folks at the Fine Arts Work Center and Atlantic Center for the Arts made my time there invaluable. Many of the scholarships I won allowed me to attend retreats in the midst of financial hardships. And for that I am humbled. And I am also grateful to all the teachers, administrators at the Squaw Valley Community of Writers. Shout out to my West Coast poetry fam! Even though I can't name you all, ya'll know who you are! And a special shout out to Cave Canem Regional workshop teachers Quincy Troupe and Patricia Spears Jones.

I cannot forget my North Cack peeps: Dr. Sheila Smith Mckoy, Wilton Barnhardt, Dr. Laura Severin, and Dr. Walt Wolfram. Each of you helped me along this journey. Much love to Carolina African American Writers' Collective (CAAWC) Co-founders Lenard Moore and Dr. Teresa Church both of you kept me grounded. And to my fellow patient MFA colleagues who graciously edited and read saw many of these first drafts Alex Distler, Keun-Hae Lee, John Michael Velez, Jake Young, J. Scott Brownlee, and William

Badger. Also much love to special friends T. Glover and K. Worth and my sorors in the South Bend Alumnae Chapter of Delta Sigma Theta, Inc. K.W.H. you make my heart soar.

And a shout out to my brand new Washington D.C. poetry community! It is a privilege to have each of you in my life and writing world. And lastly, my Morgan State University faculty and students. Some mornings, you all inspire me more than you know.

Lastly, I owe my UK family much gratitude! Jo Metcalf, the angel who saw my heart far beyond my CV. I cannot thank you enough for making the introduction. Russ Litten, you put the wind beneath the sail. Without you, this book would've never happened. Shane, you and your staff at Wrecking Ball Press have made all my dreams come true. There are no words. I curtsy again and again.

To those I may have overlooked, please forgive me. Know that your words and laughter helped carry me through. Like I said from the start, it takes a village….

celeste doaks

The thing to me about being a poet as opposed to being a playwright or a prose writer or someone who writes non-fiction, is that a poet works on several plains:

First, you have to know something about the language you work in.
Not just in a grammatical sense, but also in its possibilities, i.e. –where can it go, how can it be stretched.

Next, you have to have a feeling for music with all the stuff that involves: timing, rhythm and so forth. This is innate, of course, and can't actually be taught. You have this. Or can fool folks into thinking that you do. Honest people, clear people know the difference.

But the most important thing a poet has to have is the ability to make visible the invisible; to bring into focus and give life to that which is fleeting; peripheral; dense; and unnameable.

And that's one way that you know that the work is true even if you don't know the specifics of time and place. The poet gives voice to human stuff.

In "Cornfields and Cornrows", Celeste Doaks talks about being a wide-awake young black girl in the city I was born and grew up in: Chicago. The things she writes about: curiosity; the First lady; the passing of a beloved relative, all of these you don't have to be black female and a Southsider to know about. But what she does give that is new and fresh is sense of this life lived n the prairie, the flatlands, where there are no mountains, where everything looks placed where it is, on a grid not of your making and you look ceaselessly for the highs and the lows in a sea of metaphorical grass.

In this place, where your ancestors came from the killing fields of the plantation South looking for better life "up North", you can find yourself a symbol of the goal of that flight. And know that you have to fight even them, in the end, to come to your own self.

This book ripples like Lake Michigan, a body of water that looks like a sea. And it is tall like the skyscrapers that make up the skyline of "Chi-town".

You can read it over and over and learn new things.
Which is one of the things art does.

And what this book does, too.

Bonnie Greer

Contents

Cornrows 15
The First Time I Heard the F Word 16
Windy City Journey 17
My Last Day at Holy Cross 19
Momma Say 20
Note to Don Cornelius 22
Grandad's Two Funerals 24
Boy First, A Doaks Girl, or Daddy Say 25
First Fight at Mother Goose Nursery 27
My First Public Reading 28
God Bless the Mothers 29
Joan's Grace 30
Things I Cannot Tell my Father 31
Grandad's Stadium 33
Black Lotus 34
More Than a Love Tap 35
Watching You Eat Mango 36
For the Chef at Helios Whose Name I Did Not Know ... 37
Nigger is a Word 38
To the Sea, From Frida 39
Grocery Store, Bow Legs and a Barbie-Lady 41
Dropped Brown Egg 42
Swing Accident 43
The Interview, or Joan's Grace II 44
Learning to See 45
Friday Night at Toasty's 46
Elephant Speaks to the Dove 47

A Mother-Daughter Rite	49
Father-Daughter Time	50
Your Garden	51
Jennifer's Only Prayer	53
Ode to South Bend	55
Lunch Time at Holy Cross	56
Dear Holly Robinson, Now Peete	57
Hair Saturdays for Mrs. Lake	58
Single Twin Band Crush	60
Watching You Eat Mango II	61
The Magic Garage	62
To my Favorite Super Hero	63
Memory Before Body	64
Dad's Golf, a Foreign Language to Me	65
No Leftovers	66
On the Condition	67
Dear Dorothy/Diana	68
Call Him Anything, but	69
USA Roller Rink	70
and Cornfields	71

Cornrows

A black girl nestled between neat rows of colonial houses
begs for Black Barbies and Strawberry Shortcake dolls at Christmas,
collects *Right On!* magazines alongside Nancy Drew mysteries,
decorates her afro pigtails with ribbons and colored barrettes and
effortlessly breaks the curves in all her grade school classes because
failing isn't an option. In fact, failing is for fools!
"Grades reflect intellect" she's told as she
hopes to fulfill her father's every sober wish—
inked on a lonely white page.

Jumproping fast girls eyeball her.
Kickball kicks her ass since she's usually picked last.
Late night she rummages through momma's make up bag
mostly hoping to find pinks suitable for Molly-Ringwald lips.
No one will ever know, if she's careful.
Over in ballet class she's told her hips are unruly;
"perhaps she should find a more suitable pastime."
Quibbling about skirts that expose her bow legs,
ruined by a little brother's adoring glance she
sings the Lord's Prayer on Sunday while Grandma ushers
tired sinners to their salvation.
Underneath, the girl wonders why women don't preach in Baptist pulpits.
Vexation at early curfews and daddy's iron fist rules
wears her thin. Growing up can be such a drag!
Xenophobic might be daddy's middle name.
Yes, sometimes she wants to escape, but this
zephyr blowing in could mean a storm's brewing.

The First Time I Heard the F Word

Buckled in tight, my brown legs rest against the velvety back seat
of the eighty's black van speeding down Chapin Street. I am
a Little Miss Muffet watching the maples pass in one long smear
of green. Up front Auntie fires words at Uncle Gene and their voices
rise and fall like summer thunderstorms. Her hands flutter
on and off the steering wheel as Uncle lights a white stick,
raises it to his mouth between insults. He cranks down the window
hard with his right hand, as she rants about some woman
at Scottsdale Mall who grinned too long and called him *Geney*.
He flicks embers out his window and they fly back into mine,
spiral to the seat, burning a hole so deep the metal coils
sprang up like angered gargoyles.

Windy City Journey

Back home maple trees exist,
alongside frozen-still waters
of the St. Joseph river,
and families fist-fight in quiet
cul de sacs, while Aunt Marie
would ask momma *why
is her best friend a Polish white
girl?* But it all changed
when we crossed the state line
from Hoosierville to Illinois
headed to Jew Town,
a place where dad said
you could cop a leather jacket
for a few dollars and a good
story. Somewhere in between
Portage and Calumet
he switched the radio to BMX,
where New Edition crooned
another slow jam
and frost-covered houses—
huddled together
like smokers at break time—
slowly morphed into store-front churches
exclaiming "find Jesus today!"

Instead we found dirty Lays
chip bags; and momma complained
about the afro pics abandoned
in the streets, and that fried chicken smell
that permeated everything as we pulled
into the South Side.
What was dirt to her
was diamonds to me. CTA
busses zoomed by and black women

wearing too much make-up
and clicky heels scurried by
like a scene from *Mahogany*.
After circling multiple blocks,
Dad would get out and plunk
quarters into an awkward machine
he called a parking meter. He told us
this guaranteed we wouldn't be
ticketed for parking.
But somehow I knew
however much time
that thing gave us,
it would never be enough.

My Last Day at Holy Cross

Outside the school they argued as the sun danced
on black asphalt. Momma's nostrils flared as she spoke
to the nun in short staccato phrases. *But she's not stupid.*
Sometimes she gets flustered. At age six, flustered didn't compute
but I knew my troubled tongue was the problem. During reading class
those Nan and Ted sentences stuck in my mouth like grains of salt, clogged
in a shaker that fell out in clumps, or sometimes not at all.
But this stutterer listened close until Miss Mary Mack,
complete with white collar, said things I did understand. *She's holding*
back the rest of class. Perhaps she should stay behind. Her voice chilled
with ice cubes while momma stayed hot as a furnace. And often
I stood—my mouth buttoned shut—the same way I did in ballet class.
My brown feet posed in some strange configuration, arms open,
slightly bent at the elbows as if asking for a hug. This is how I learned
every dance; how I learned my positions.

Momma Say

i keep sayin' her name
half in awe, half in disbelief
i keep sayin' her name over
and over like some broken ol' 45
record. And sometimes she looks at me
like she knows i been waitin' for her
all my life and her grandmomma say
she an old soul, but i say she
a firecracker cause what girlchile
you know take 28 hours to birth?
what girlchile you know scream
like she got whole sentences to say
the minute she born? that's my girl
born wit a head fulla coal black curls
that must be from her daddy's side since
mine's fulla buckshots and her
skin feel like tissue paper and
sometimes i worry if i pick her
up too quickly, she might break
so mostly i just stare, and worry
if she's eatin' enough
or eatin' too much i worry if
she should sleep on her stomach
or more on her back
i worry if she's too warm or cold
or if those baby booties itch her
tiny feet, but most of all i worry
my husband and his damn cancer sticks
pollutin' the air she breathe
now i done tole him to go outside
if he gotta puff those things
but who can tell a man
what to do in his own house?
i shouldn't, but i do, cause i hafta.

cain't have my only piece of heaven
all stuffed up   cause if she is
he's gonna see my backside permanently
i love him-i really do-
but this baby girl love just stops you
in your tracks and make you grin
even if you only caught a note
of her Motown magic

Note to Don Cornelius

1

Soul Train was all the rage when I was little. Black folks paraded
on stage in jumpsuits, bell bottoms and stacked boots; their afros picked
out into the cosmos. While we Midwesterners wondered, *California, how
did you do it? How'd you make the zoot suit so cool?* We envied your
eternal sunsets, coastline kissing the Pacific, and most of all your train.

2

        The Soul Train. That big choo choo
                      blessing our TV screens
           telling us to go west and be free.
But it was always your baby Don,
            the black boy from Bronzeville,
    Chicago's infamous South Side.
  You traded in your uniform for wide
            collars and plaid polyester pants.
         An ex-Marine who served your country
and then us. Made your dollars selling
          cars and insurance policies 'til you got called
to the big screen's pulpit. And despite
        your own battles, you brought the King
     of Pop and the Godfather of Soul
  to a wide-eyed nation of rhythmic hearts.
    It was you Don, the scramble board—
        and a Chinese girl whose name
           we'd never know, her hair a cascade
        of black waist-length snakes—
  that made us all want to pop and lock forever.

3

And what do we do now
after hearing you put the gun
to chin, surrendering
to the rush of steel and cracked skull?
What do we do now
that you've gone on to greet
the angels and frolic with all
the other greats? Oh Don,
when we ascend to that final
resting parlor upstairs, will you
share your secrets
of how to wear the mask with panache?
Sometimes when it cracks, we want it to;
giving the world a peek at humanity
and blackness undone. Don, will you
tell us what ever happened
to that scramble board and where
we might find our next sunset?

Grandad's Two Funerals

1

In South Bend the robed choir sang sappy hymns,
while the minister spoke politely about going home
to the Lord. People dabbed their eyes as if
they were in an ICU full of newborns, and I still fumed
from a fight with dad where he blamed my lateness
on getting all dolled up like my mother. The family limo
outside waiting impatiently for me.

2

But in Trenton, Tennessee even the air tasted different.
No fancy limos, dad and I didn't butt heads,
and my brother and I rode silently to Mount Olive
Baptist church with the windows peeled down,
humidity in our throats, and Tupac's *Shed So Many Tears*
looping in the tape deck. I wore open toed sandals
and a thin rayon dress, as my brother took swigs
from a Remy Martin bottle stashed under the driver's seat.
It clinked when we turned sharp corners. Inside the church
a top-heavy black woman with a bad weave and tacky pumps,
her feet oozing over the sides, belted out *His Eye Is On The Sparrow*.
Those notes were daggers in my ears as dad's feet stamped
so furiously making me think the ground might open
its jaws, devouring him and momma.
She was his delicate bodyguard, a pillar that only turned
when the preacher and family members finished reciting
their memories and comical antidotes.

And eventually Dad, Uncle Tommy, and six of granddad's brothers
lined up in two rows, the bumble bees circling their freshly cut heads,
faces heavy with sweat and tears, and carried Granddad's body
right out of that church like eight shiny-suited black Cadillacs headed
home.

Boy First, A Doaks Girl, or Daddy Say

Now my mind was all set on Eric or Anthony or Raymond
    and I get a girl. I mean, how many basketball games can you play
        with a girl? Can't show her no free throw shots, can't toss her

a Walter Payton ball, can't show her how to scrub the white walls
    clean as a nickel whistle with a brillo pad when she's washing my ride—
        cause girls ain't inta that. She'll probably be like her momma, hell

she already screams and cries a lot. She'll probably like shopping
    just like her too. Spend whole days lookin' at them stores and comin' home
        with fancy smellin' perfumes and too-short skirts. Well, I won't

have it. She gonna do as I say, go to college and keep her dress down.
    She can't gimme that look, like the one she givin' me now,
        expectin' me to melt. No sir-ree. She can't have everything

she want just cause she cute. And that she is. Popcorn curly hair
    like my father and dimples like me. But that don't change the fact—
        she's still a girl. A Doaks girl. Got my blood in her but hopefully

she don't turn out to be a smoker like me. Or a drinker.
    In fact, I'm gonna come home early on Fridays, steada drinkin'
        with the boys at the bowlin' alley. Wellll maybe I'll have,

one or two. Just cause imma a new father don't mean I gotta stop
    everything, now do it? But I do plan to cut back on the cigarettes,
        maybe take more walks. Maybe take her wit me. Ride her around

in one of those fancy strollers—she'd like that.
    But damn what would I do if we out and she start that cryin'?
        Good thing her momma has her mosta the day. I'm not too good

at that shit. I mean, how am I supposta know if she hungry
 or sleepy or angry? See how she squirmin' now? Her face all mashed up
  like potatoes, like she gone cry. Maybe she know I was expectin'

someone who could carry my name. Maybe she know
 Southern folks like me believe
  that birthin' a boy first is good luck.

First Fight at Mother Goose Nursery

I hated this new prayer, this
one nation under god, indivisible, being shoved into my mouth
without permission. And the saying of it confused me. Plus
momma always preached "don't repeat things you don't
understand." So my lips were clamped shut
despite this small ivory boy, who was no more than snails
and puppy dog tails to me, urging me to say it. Yes, I knew and liked
as we forgive those who trespass against us, but when I refused to utter
this new grace, his flamed and coiled fingers swung, landing with a thud
in my belly. Years later I would forever remember this judge and jury,
this criminal and copper. He would always be the first bright white boulder
crashing into this dark pool, with liberty and justice for none.

My First Public Reading

I loved living, neatly folded, under Ms. Kuester's
various bell-shaped, A-lined, and pleated skirts.

Those colorful checkered, solid, and print frocks were more 'lived in'
than my parents' house. Below the folds of my teacher's skirt I was free

from ridicule and names like "teacher's pet";
"four eyes", repeated too many times for my ears.

At lunchtime I'd pen short stories, and the occasional poem
which she'd read and quickly extol "How innovative"!

Those times were like rubies to me, as if my classmates
disappeared in a puff of magic smoke.

Cloaked beneath Ms. Kuester's skirt, nothing could hurt me
and math equations seem to solve themselves.

Grammar turned into *Wheel of Fortune* and she
became our Vanna White, gently turning the letters.

From my hiding place the view was funny.
Her skirt, a large circus tent, the children, performing animals

I'd want to play with but lions, and tigers, and fears
froze my feet solid. Until one day,

towards the end of 6th grade, she decided to scoot me
out of my cozy home asking, "Won't you read your story aloud for the
class?"

And that day I stood and read, heavy words falling
from my mouth, her skirt's wool loose 'round my ankles.

God Bless the Mothers

God bless the mothers who think
your only problem is the termites
making their daily meals from
pine planks that shield the house's skin.
Mothers who cringe at the smell
of fertilizer feeding your ragged lawns,
and shut the windows at the first whiff.
God bless you as you pack smashed eggs
and ground beef together for tonight's meatloaf
hoping last week's saltines haven't lost their crunch
in the cabinet. *Bless* your sons cloaked in Bad Boy
tracksuits and bright white kicks as they toil away
in indigo-bathed bedrooms over plastic bags.
God bless mothers who slave over the stove's eye
while your sons double check a steel scale
watching the needle teeter back and forth
with that stop-traffic red hand. *God,*
your sons' slender fingers could be shrink-wrapping
their lives away. *God bless*. And mothers, the heavy lines
beneath your eyes should rings alarms,
sounding to the world, that your sons are
lured by another sound: the muted non-stop buzz
of their cell phones and the chamber's click
that will silence whatever hunger
tonight's dinner cannot feed.

Joan's Grace

"What did I know, what did I know of love's austere and lonely offices?"
Robert Hayden

Joan, my 4th grade friend,
whose tattered clothes were hand-me-downs
from her aunt's and uncle's older children,
was loads better than Lisa, whose black-framed glasses
sat on her face like an old building about to collapse, or Sean,
the mocha-colored boy who pushed me off all slides
and swings at recess, grinning assiduously afterwards.
Or even Sammy, the ivory girl who stuttered more
than I did when nervous.

In the mornings before school, I would see Joan
leading her mom by the hand, the guide dog directing
the father, both of them swimming in a world of darkness,
as they stooped down to place lips on their daughter's cheek.

Now I think how silly most of us were, embarrassed
to wear the wrong OshKosh B'Gosh jeans,
of a parent dropping us off too close to the front door.

That's when her grace occurs to me, the school bell
chiming just before three, and her running outside
to greet her parents as they stood,
both pairs of eyes staring aimlessly
into a sea of children waiting
for Joan's familiar touch,
or the comforting timbre
of her voice.

Things I Cannot Tell my Father
~for poet Aaron Smith

I think golf is boring because grown men chasing
a tiny white ball seems juvenile to me.
Your cologne mix of Jovan Musk and Old Spice for Men
makes me nauseous.
I always loved your grin.
I drink too much because of you.
Normally when I call the house I ask for mom
because talking to you is awkward.
I've touched myself in your house.
I occasionally smoke because of you.
But at least I don't smoke
your obscure Vantage Green brand.
I wonder if you're a good lover to mom.
I believe I'm good at pool because that's one of the few
measurable things you taught me.
I'm a perfectionist because you came home from the army full of orders.
I left home at 17 and rarely return because of you.
I remember when you said *it will be hard for you to date*
with your hair that way.
I've smoked weed and enjoyed it.
I know that you've smoked weed and enjoyed it.
I love your sister's wit and intelligence and often wonder how
you two came from the same two parents.
I think my difficulty loving men stems from my difficulty loving you.
You take too long to bathe.
I saw your underwear too often when I was young.
I see you going to church now and think *he's a reformed sinner*.
I don't understand how you captured my mother's heart back then.
I fart and giggle about it.
I hate driving with you because a long time ago you mentioned
all women drivers are pathetic.
I stole your shoehorns out of your Florsheim shoes.
I cried at Granddad's funeral because I felt more for your loss than mine.

I hate how you wake up when I change the channel saying *hey,
I was watching that.*
I hate how you lied to us about our half-brother.
I hate how you made mom suffer.
I once told mom to leave you.
Despite my anger, I still want the reason you grin to be
because of who I turned out to be.

Grandad's Stadium

On Johnson Street, it was a pie in my face, this game.
Daily, the parlor room transformed into a stadium for the game.

The Cubs verses the Sox, everyone's favorite warring Chicagos.
All jock and chinstraps, their manhood forever a race in the game.

Grandad's house became a boob tube respite where
graying black men gathered to watch the pace of the game.

Donning suspenders they'd chat and beer and puff up the room,
hoping to glimpse Ernie Banks' face in the game.

My tiny ears glued to their gripes and their grumbles:
AD, who struck out? Who just stole second base in the game?

Nothing could rival the buzz of last minute home runs,
Not even a celestial toddler cooing for love, a disgrace in the game.

Black Lotus
Dedicated to Michelle Obama

Lotus rising out of South Side water & night
Gifting the world with your brilliant fruitful flower
We marvel at your beauty; bless your seeds with light

You bloom ivy, league that is, grow tall in their sight
Defying every shallow pond with fierce power
Lotus rising out of South Side water & night

Your floral family hails from a deep southern plight
Ancestors fertilize the A.M.E. church hour
We marvel at your beauty; bless your seeds with light

For three days your petals bloom gallant as a knight
Picture that - Monet paints you in sun or shower
Lotus rising out of South Side water & night

How many six foot stalks revel in their rare height?
Dark pods don't flinch; stand stoic as a light tower
We marvel at your beauty; bless your seeds with light

Stem of Third World Center, Egyptians know your rite
We pray you never wane or retreat to bower
Lotus rising out of South Side water & night
We marvel at your beauty; bless your seeds with light

More Than a Love Tap

At sixteen his flirting was always wrapped
in snarky comments and eyerolls, but today
his love came hurdled in a newspaper flying
towards my stoop. He pitched sports and weather
and murder at me from our concrete walkway.
The bases were loaded as this paper flew
towards home plate, and after smacking the back
of my head, my feet set fire to neighboring lawns
crushing pampas grass, up-rooting otherwise dry
brown earth. And *damn* if I wasn't gaining on him,
rounding Johnson Street, approaching the emerald hill
behind the Cogdell's house. That's when
I spotted him— nothing but a pinkish-ivory blur—dashing
for his Datsun. Just as I'm about to yell *you pasty piece of shit*,
the whole world slows—like that scene
out of "Carlito's Way"
when Charlie tries
to catch that train,
panting with panic, with Gail
only a stair-step away—
then my knee buckles with a dull snap.
I'm yelling, descending to the ground,
maple trees and cape cods all swirling,
my painful screams mixed with the chirps of cardinals.

Watching You Eat Mango
~for DeAvery Irons

is like being in a threesome since
every minute the volcanoes of me
are constantly erupting. I am an outlet
filled with too many plugs, gazing
at you that first time on the bed
with her. My nose hairs tickle with
the sweet smell of you and this new thing.
My mouth craves your fingers dripping wet
with her juices as you tear into the soft
orange flesh. So with all this distraction,
how's a girl to know where to place
her attention? I give up, give in and when
we are all finished, and the sheets sworn
to secrecy, I leave bereft of vowels,
a new language burning on my tongue.

For the Chef at Helios Whose Name I Do Not Know

The conversation starts with peanut butter, as the guy with
wire-rimmed glasses grabs the stool next to me, asking if I enjoyed
my PBJ sandwich. His sapphire blue pools almost distract me
before I begin to critique it in classic Virgo style. It was too grainy
and wasn't sweet enough. *And did I taste a hint of cinnamon?*
Meanwhile, my eye catches a robin building a nest just outside
the glass window of Helios. He places sticks, sordid pieces of cloth
and debris bit by bit into a cone shape. The robin is unafraid
to build what may not hold, as we, two strangers, teeter
towards connection. Steam rises from new lattes, and fingers tap
laptops constructing lines of nothingness. As our chat comes
to a close he admits he's the chef that makes the peanut butter
fresh everyday. Oh saintly chef, you do this daily never knowing
if or when anyone will ever eat it until someone like me arrives,
orders your labor of love, devours the sandwich, and then analyzes it
like a term paper. How many of us never stop to think about your hands
shelling the nuts one by one, gently blending the oil into crunchy pulp.
Each step so delicate, so purposeful, like a beak pushing
each twig into it's perfect position.

Nigger is a Word

that sits on your plate for decades,
an uneaten vegetable
no one wants,
like zucchini or an eggplant,
whose bruised purple skin
is a constant embarrassment.
Even children know
how bad it tastes,
so when Melissa spit it at me,
pushed the word onto my
3rd grade menu, I held on
to its rottenness, tasted
its stench, rolled it around.
A dull, lifeless flavor in my mouth.

To the Sea, from Frida
~ inspired by Frida Kahlo's "Memory" painting

this brown tweed jacket
sprinkled with cinnamon splotches
the black buttons that choke my wrists
cloak an immaculate white dress
underneath, my body gutted like a trout
my skin, barely recognizable
carefully stitched together
i am a colorful, useless quilt
of delicate bones cradled
in plaster corsets
their white teeth gnawing at my meat
my pin cushion full of nails
holding together a house of sand
that slowly sifts out to sea
where my heart should be
a hole exists
bleeds blood-red tides
that ebb only when Diego
touches me
this pulmonary vessel sails
underneath a sunless grey blue sky
as i live between two worlds
the girl of my youth
who curtseyed with ankle socks
full of grown up dreams
mixed with the fractured woman
who stands before you now
one foot on land
and the other greeting the sea gods
who will hopefully
devour these breasts
which are mounds of broken magic
sexless balloons filled with rancid air

that scare even the softest touch
i ask the sea to swallow
this stabbed pelvis
drink my burgundy soil
sea, deliver me whole
and not forever hanging
on this clothesline of life

Grocery Store, Bow Legs and a Barbie-Lady

"How does it feel to be a problem?" W.E.B. Du Bois

My eight-year-old ears craved the *ding* when
Kreamo bread slid over the scanner. They perked up
at the crunch of chip bags, the bagger boy's timbre
over the loud speaker, and momma's pen scratching down
the latest dinner list. My hands loved to hold the cartoonish
cereal boxes as I rode high in metal shopping carts,
whizzing by cookie-cutter housewives with their
baskets of bologna. So when an older Barbie-lady came over
questioning my then too-curvy legs and corrective shoes,
momma shook her permed coif back and forth, wincing.
This was her attempt to shield me from knifey words
knowing sticks and stones can break anyone; and just as I was about
to utter the tiniest **hi**, something rendered me silent as the swallow.

Dropped Brown Egg

"Everything becomes public in a small town."
from *Funes the Memorious* by Jorge Luis Borges

Without the tiny scar on my right arm to remind me,
nothing would reel me back to that humid June day
when the air stood and did not move. Momma was busy
scrambling daddy's royal breakfast and Old Spice snuck out
the bathroom door where daddy put the blade to face. That day I was
assigned to mind baby brother; and I arm-cradled him
on the front porch, bouncing him knee to knee, dreaming
of a taffy-colored baby girl. She would be my caramel icing,
my symphony of sugar. But when I awoke he was splayed
on concrete cracked and oozing, a brown egg frying,
sizzling so loud that momma flew from the kitchen,
and daddy's shaving cream plopped to the ground,
a fallen white cloud, as he switched my one guilty limb.

Swing Accident

Underneath a too hot sun, and strict orders from momma,

    we headed out to Marquette Park, my big right hand gripping

his tiny left one. If the brother was a sister perhaps we could be

    playing Barbies, or sniffing the sweetness of Strawberry Shortcake,

but instead we were trotting down the grassy knoll.

He dashed for the slide, colored sad as a gray sky, while I headed

for the metal swings. I loved to pump, shooting high, my fingers clutched

    around the chain-links, my feet happily dangling, until a brown blur

crossed the dusty sand. How did my feet became a tirade of punches

    landing on top of his cranium and eardrums? How did his face become

    a thud, underneath my gummed sneakers? Wordless among his screams,

I launched off the swing to tend to my brother, his nose gushing blood,

the seat left dangling like my dream of a sister, the dust still bustling up,

    rocks spewing everywhere. Everything still clouding my view.

The Interview, or Joan's Grace II

I'm sure the reporter thought us to be rogues, the worst
types of human beings, a selfish couple of handicaps.
Although I could not see his wincing or even his furrowed
eyebrow, the tone cloaking his questions gave him away.

> *Were you worried that the infant would*
> *be born blind too? How did you and your wife meet?*
> *The first few months, were they difficult?*

I answered them all, as Ann Marie rubbed
my knee. Her rhythmic hand a kind of salve
for my imbuing anger. Yes, we were worried,
and of course the first few months were hell,
but aren't they for most parents? I didn't add
how we had all her clothes folded and sectioned
by the fabric's textures, or how we knew by heart
where the knob should point on the stove
for perfect milk-warming. And he'd never believe
how Joanie's mouth instinctively found
my wife's nipple. And for his finale he would inquire:

> *Did you ever think about abortion, or about giving her up*
> *for adoption to a more capable family?*

I hesitate to answer, as Ann shifts on our worn
couch, a slight sigh escaping her mouth, like a
balloon flailing to the ground.

Learning to See

A short package of brown,
my pigtails punctuated
with ribbons momma color-coordinated
against my will, I arrived cheesing
at Mrs. Pappas' heavy classroom door,
as she donned a decisive frown.

Glasses weren't wearing me
yet, but already things were starting
to get fuzzy. Numbers on the wall
clock, assignments chalked on
blackboards, and even my tiny
shoestrings, unless they were inches
from my face. This was my introduction
to nearsightedness.

I remember momma
dragging me to the place I couldn't
pronounce Op-TOM-e-trist
and sitting in that stiff, overgrown chair
attempting to read the black letters,
neatly-rowed against the background,
stark white as cotton. It was as difficult
as reading Mrs. Pappas' face, a block of concrete
as I arrived excited that first day of class,
my Wonder Woman lunch pail
hanging from my grasp.

After getting my new spectacles, I remember
running outside amazed at how each
individual leaf, serrated or lobed,
seemed to be waving green
on the maples overhead. Later in life
I would recall Mrs. Pappas' frown,
her distaste for me and my kind
slowly coming into focus.

Friday Nights at Toasty's

Most Friday nights my family careened down Michigan Street
in Dad's Chrysler Cordoba, a makeshift pimp car.
The open windows ushered in a brisk breeze that blew
daddy's militant afro, screaming towards a deaf sky, as we slid
into a parking space. The neon sign burning red as hot sauce.

Inside Toasty's the perfectly pale waitresses wore
throwback Fifties skirts and rouge smiles. One would eventually
sashay us to a pleather booth where my tan legs stuck
to the seats. And most nights momma would balk about fingerprints
on water glasses while the table's jukebox blared
UB40's "Red, Red Wine". Before dinner arrived
my assignment was to score a quarter, flip the knob,
and scan for a rare Whitney or Michael among the hundreds
of titles. This continued until red lips and skirt appeared
with my meal: ivory shrimps wrapped in fried ochre coating.
The bread crumbs melted against my naïve tongue
and I never could recall momma and daddy's meals, just their
desserts. All I can remember is how the other families never
looked like us and momma and daddy would always split
what seemed like the only root beer float in all of Toasty's.

Elephant Speaks to the Dove

Frida Kahlo was often referred to by her friends as "the dove"; and Diego Rivera, her husband, was sometimes called an elephant due to his heavy stature.

Carino, your dreams did not die
in the bow of that school bus
a silent canary coming to pierce
your spine   pelvis   collarbone
but no derailed thief
could steal your proud guerilla reds
you pray for death
but i save your breaths on a spindle
weave airy wool as you slumber
tuck them like socks in our armoire
that i will someday read
to our three children whose cheeks
will never know our kisses
your body is not broken
but rather a delicate vase
of cracked glass that
smiles under Coyoacan *sol*
sits on my heart's shelf
devoid of flowers
but glorious in its own emptiness
i know pain splits your body
like a lightning bolt
its electric currents driving you
to bottles of Patron
the liquor a salve for your
bleeding soul
you worship painkillers
and the paintbrush, they become
your only God
and i do not help matters much

with my disobedient penis
poking the pistils of other flowers
lo siento mi amor
but when i gaze at you
draped in ornate Tehuacán dress
flawed and flawless
debilitated and divine
your mouth full of four letter abrasions
how you prepare my lunches
while i labor over luxurious murals
how your bird-like hands bathe
this elephant body
i am nothing but grateful
your white wings have descended
on me with fire and *alegria*

A Mother-Daughter Rite

Because momma's a germophobe — a woman
obsessed with a dishless kithen sink, spot-free glass
tables, and clean vaginas — she taught me how
to toilet paper the seat in the public stalls
of rest stops, airports, diners, and all the places
grown ladies put a bright tube of red to lips before
leaving the mirror. Somewhere around age five I remember
lifting up my dress and slip and pausing, for her
to show me the process. *You've got to pull it down
real steady, like this, so it won't crinkle. Then measure
four squares each, two long ones, for the left and right sides,
and then a third, shorter one, which you'll double-fold,
for the middle—it's the most important.* With each layer she
moved gracefully, a ballet dancer over the commode, not stirring
any wind that might send the makeshift seat to the tile floor.
All the while humming a hymn from last Sunday's
church service. Watching her hands secure the white covering,
I wondered how many other daughters were shown
this rite. How many other mother's went
through all this to protect the Y, this hidden secret,
between their daughters legs?

Father-Daughter Time

"Everything is holy! everybody's holy! everywhere is holy! everyday is in eternity! Everyman's an angel!" Allen Ginsberg

was his ritual of running water in a red plastic bucket, the shammy,
and the Palmolive with its emerald green tint. Our Saturday afternoons,
he would always take me, the oldest girl, out back to scrub the grime.
The layer of dust, thin as a spiderweb, from being at the paint factory
during the days, and at the Why Not pub nights the garage was empty.
Oh what a blessing to watch his hands working, wiping the hood
clean to perfection, the same way a carpenter sands two wooden planks
into a seamless dream. Even the raised chrome got special attention,
the way I wished my announcements of another "A" would elicit
a grin. But instead, this was our father-daughter time.
His kneeling on one knee, hands baptized
in suds, scrubbing the sapphire paint spotless,
asking me to Brillo-pad the whitewalls.
He stressed their importance, saying
they must be as pristine as the tablecloth
at the last supper.

Your Garden
~For Grandad AD before Lung Cancer

outside in back fiery tomatoes hang
like bowling balls
off tiny vines
Granny Smiths peer
down at you
their tart faces
full of disdain
bald onions sit next to
hairy peaches
but neither gets green of the other
poised peas wait patiently
knowing, they would soon be snapped
and sometimes collard greens
have holes in their stockings
but we grandkids eat them nonetheless

inside darkness reigned
and light tiptoed around
in respect of its elder
ancient grime smiled
on stove and kitchen sinks
in your barely living
room sat your favorite shit
brown leather chair
with lumpy arm rests
like womanly breasts
it always faced the idiot box
where usually your Cubs were on
they always did excite you
more than me
and on your nightstand
Grandmomma's picture sat

stationary
perhaps she watched from her grave
as you dug yours
the walls closing in
the cigar smoke devouring you
the back garden gallantly growing
despite your decision to die

Jennifer's Only Prayer
~in the voice of Pryor's fourth and last wife

Richard, you were my whole world
spinning black and beautiful
you were the grease sizzle
when the chicken hits the pan
a James Brown split
neckbones and collard greens
the reason why we said "crib" insteada house
the watusi, be-bop, A Love Supreme
and Naima on repeat forever
you were JoJo Dancing
us into the 80's
you were Gene Wilder's Laurel and Hardy
you brought us the mirror and begged us
to look at our visage
you held down the mirror and snorted
the white lady like she was going out of style
you said "That nigger's crazy" and of course,
you were
you set yourself and us on fire
you came to this world burning hot
as a lit cigarette next to a mansion fulla kerosene
you were our brightest nebula
a complex quasar always headed for infamy
you were the reason to fuck up, laugh
about it on stage, and move on
the child of an unwed mother raised in
your grandmother's brothel
born unto things your eyes couldn't
digest and because of that
rage found your fists and your fists
eventually found my jaw, but still
you were my atomic bomb of brilliance

with the gentle heart of butterfly wings
you were my abuser, a manic-depressive,
a shit-talking womanizer who
paced the stage like a caged panther
your face twitching and contorting
eyes bulging spraying our
darkest secrets on your public canvas

Richard, even as you sat there
your wit gagged and bound
by the wheelchair
the Multiple Sclerosis creeping up,
dulling your mind's blade
your muscles bowing their heads to
death's bright light
you would always be my
phoenix rising
my black Superman
my volcano of words
my orange moon
my kiss in the rain
my only prayer to heaven and hell

Ode to South Bend

Oh how I loved the taste of you
as I bit into your gigantic cakey O's
of frosting at Dainty Maid bakery.
And my tongue still remembers how
your Claey's dark Chocolate Charlie
christened plates at Christmastime
or slid down my throat at New Year's.
Who could deny anything fried, seared or baked
from Toasty's restaurant on Main Street,
the parking lot littered with families
that never looked like ours.
South Bend, I even adored the look of you
your potholes on Portage avenue, your snaked
electrical lines with icicles hanging down
like daggers. You were beautiful
in any hue so I couldn't wait to pedal
my pink Huffy over to Grandad's house
or to the Burger Dairy corner store where
colorful nickel candies would sparkle and wink
when I entered. South Bend, I even loved
the factory of you when mom, dad, and I
would cruise past all those bricked places
that housed the men in my family. You birthed
the original Studebaker and Bendix Corporation
where thousands of car brakes were pumped out
lubing the spokes of General Motors.
While the Fuller O'Brien company painted
your streets and signed my father's checks for years.
So how could I not love you South Bend
your sweet smelling Kreamo bread factory
always luring me near? South Bend, sometimes,
just sometimes I wish those doughy smoke plumes,
billowing like mini-gods, would have skewed my view
of our Johnson Street home littered with spray paint
and signs that stuck out like dandelions
reading *Leave, nigger leave.*

Lunch Time at Holy Cross

The carton was the culprit that slipped, falling that September day
from her fingers at lunch time, the milk inside spilling
its shiny eggshell white across hardwood floors, scattering
nosy school kids like a broken strand of pearls. It wasn't
the ham sandwich sliced perfectly in half, the chips, raisins,
or one Archway cookie momma packed, that sent the little gems
rolling away as black shoes and habit stormed back
to the liquid mess. The nun unleashed a tongue-lashing as if the girl
was a baa baa black sheep. She had no wool but perhaps silliness
should be her defense; anything to make sense of this punishment.
The girl left alone, kneeling down, scrubbing the floor and her brown self
against the ivory grime.

Dear Holly Robinson, Now Peete

The camera's in love with you, and so was I, along with thousands
of other pre-adolescent black girls. Our hormones thru the roof,
Double A bras in tow. Focused, the lens was transfixed on your
pouty mouth and mane, curly and thick. And to tell the truth,
we were elated that among all the guy cops, you were the lone girl,
dipped in chocolate. You hugged Penhall with cool reserve
and joked easy with Hansen, were unconcerned with purses or pearls.
Gorgeous as an African violet, Holly, *Officer Judy Hoffs*, dame with steel nerves
did you know we existed on the other side of the lens? Every Sunday our lives
hung on your every scripted line. We envied your eye-shadow flaming blue,
banana-clipped ponytails, and unsolved cases. The way you all slapped
   high-fives.
And who cared if your father was Gordon from Sesame Street? We knew
it was you Holly, that kept all of us hushed on shag green carpet, sitting
   Indian-style.
You were our Hollywood diva showing us we could go the distance, even
   multiple miles.

Hair Saturdays for Mrs. Lake

Saturdays mom would load me up
in dad's blue Cutlass Supreme
and drive over to the side of town
where the men would stand curbside
in polyester pants or work jeans,
the long white cigarettes dangling
out their mouths like apologies.
But I would suffer anything
to become beautiful, straight and silky-haired.
Mrs. Lake lived on Walnut Street where
houses huddled close enough that you could hear
neighbors peeing, wiping, *and* flushing.
She was an elderly black woman whose own
silvery strands screamed of oil and the hot comb.
She'd press me in that dark,
dank basement smelling of her cats
Rinny and Nelly, the ceilings so low
they might French kiss her customers.
And she chewed dip, kept a white paper cup
filled with brown spit, worrisome to watch
but I did. This was the sacrifice made, penance
paid, to leave looking as fine as wine.

> She would dip her thumb,
> pointer finger in oil
> slick the strand
> rescue hot comb from stove
> then press sizzle
> press sizzle

This was the cadence I'd come to memorize
until one day momma confessed
Mrs. Lake was sick. Then, Saturdays passed

with no sorry men whispering low
and no visit to Walnut Street
but somehow on weekends I always longed
for the typical Saturday routine of thumb,

        pointer finger
        dip in oil
        slick the strand
        grab the hot comb from the stove
        then press sizzle
        press sizzle

Single Twin Band Crush
~dedicated to Joe Millar

Aaron and Anita, the first real twins I ever personally knew,
drum majored our ragged band in high school called—
the Marching LaSalle Lions. Anita was the outgoing,
mouthy one, but I was star-struck by Aaron, the brooder.

I adored his strange pink olivey skin—always tan,
even in bitter Midwest winters—and his black spiked hair.
Of course those were the late 80's, and the whole world reeled
from Reaganomics, bad pop icons like Robert Palmer and his red-lipped
dames, and the Challenger crashed down on us like hail pelting
car hoods. Even my parents cautiously skated on the thin ice
of their marriage. No music could change America's forecast then.

But when Aaron coached me on flute, he calmed this confusing
world. He was the one who taught me the crescendos and intermezzos
of John Philip Sousa. As the world stammered on off-beat,
he was the one teaching me delicate rhythms
of quarter & eighths marching on regardless.

Watching You Eat Mango II

As you chewed, questions dripped
from corners of your mouth. Who knows
when it will happen, or how? Could be
as you remove my one lonesome sock
from the dryer for the 40th time,
or after washing another one of my
half-drank cups of green tea. (You always
hated my commitment to antioxidants.)
But somehow, as you ripped the flesh free
from the fruit's smooth rind, sweetness
was already evaporating. Your molars
and bicuspids grinding down on truth,
your tongue feeling the pieces,
and the morning light falling 'round
my shoulders like a sad new discovery.

The Magic Garage

The garage behind Aunt Juanita's small two-bedroom house
on Ohio Street seemed shrouded in gold dust when I was little. Most Fridays
it was filled with dad and my uncles, taller to me than Rodin's shadow.
Sometimes, against momma's objections, I'd sneak out and peep at them
through the open door, staring awestruck at all the men in my family.
Most of them had nicknames as if they were strange superheroes.
Uncle Tommy was Uncle Wine, no explanation needed. Uncle Luther
Became Bud and Dad was Rock—the hardest one to crack during a game
of Five-card stud. Jack or Jim Beam filled their glasses as they cursed
blue magic. Pants pulled up to their knees, country-style. Nowadays, I wish
that dust existed, was real enough to protect these men who drank too much
and the women they stumbled home to. The little girl in me still savors
this scene, the jokes, and the infamous hollering. The woman
that girl grew into now blesses those playing cards
slapping down on the table like pieces
of a broken, azure sky.

To my Favorite Super Hero
~ for Linda Cordova Carter

Screw the indestructible bracelets
repelling bullets at each sway and turn.

Forget the Lasso of Truth that renders
male villains to their knees. Erase her undying love

for Steve Trevor. With no Nazi takeovers
or pressing justice to defend what remains?

Cascades of black tresses, dark third-world eyes,
a generous helping of hips, and her long legs luring us all to the border.

Would she be our shero if you found her
two buxom breasts cloaked by a fuzzy robe,

her body hoisted over a pot of beans and rice,
stirring occasionally while awaiting her children's return from school?

Would she be so revered if people knew
those tight red boots were just a moonlight from domestic work?

Would the mop and broom be as glorious
as the clownish costume drooping from a back closet hangar?

Memory Before Body

"If there is a history then I do not own it." Ross Gay

Childhood scents are the rungs of a ladder we climb everyday
of our adult lives. We remember to climb gently, each footstep
recalling momma's chocolate chip cookies at Christmastime,
or the tinge of bleach wafting through the air from a freshly-mopped
kitchen floor. Or maybe a father's piney sawdust just beyond
the garage door hinge. These ghosts we greet each morning
waking to daylight falling through blinds. The apparitions the nose knows.

Even now, a crimson spray paint can perched right outside
my brownstone window conjures his after-five arrival from O'Brien's.
The reek of fumes comes back, his blue work-coat soiled as he peeked
throughout the house for me. But before his afro and steel-toe boots
    would appear,
turpentine, thinner, and solvent were there. Before he could round
the corners of our stucco walls, I held his whole day inside my lungs.
The heated words cast down from white superiors, the lunch banter of men,
the thousands of hours gone by waiting for the minute-hand to cross over
    to five.

Dad's Golf, a Foreign Language to Me

Before Tiger, his Cablinasian identity, straying penis,
and prestigious green jacket, there was dad dragging me
Erskine to practice. His attempt to show his daughter
the difference between a 9-iron and a Driver.

The lesson began with his rough factory hands maneuvering
my ankles, *the stance is the key* he would say. Then he'd babble
more stuff I didn't understand: *It's tough to land a ball
on the green and you should avoid the sand!*

While I dreamed of a bucket and shovel, kids frolicking,
a makeshift starfish or seashell.

The session would continue like this, the other men staring
because I was the wrong color wrong gender,
and my father caring less. His only objective
was to speak his foreign language, as I tried hard
to comprehend what bogies and double eagles were.
Was a five-iron like a high-five? Could anyone tell me
if sudden death would make me sick?

Inside, I begged to be free
of these lessons; sometimes, just sometimes
in between the pauses where dad's eyes would glaze over,
while reminiscing about Lee Elder, I would become
that graceful white Spalding soaring high over all those
waving flags, somehow always headed for greener fairways.

No Leftovers

Sometimes momma disguised last night's baked chicken
in a casserole or a fancy stir-fry since everyone knew
daddy, the military man, didn't do day-old, freezer-burned anything.
He always sniffed out leftovers like a dusty grenade hidden
in deep foreign soil. Even if the plates and silverware shone
like new money his wrinkled brow, or sullen frown, trained me
to understand that fresh is always best. So momma taught me how
to please a man, this man, my father, through his stomach.
And here began my training as a mini-sous chef, everyday
snapping the peas, shucking bushels of Grandad's garden corn,
my six-year-old legs dangling off that mustard yellow kitchen chair,
everything a warning; the husks and silks revealing tender kernels,
the leafy green shells floating into a paper bag of airy nothingness.

On the Condition
~for Uncle Thomas

If I could've asked you to hold on to life back then, maybe
I wouldn't be perched on this stool now, clutching a glass
of your old standby, Seagram's, wishing I could've told you
not to sip that last shot before entering the sedan,
the steel doors squeaking like pigs going to slaughter.

If I could I would've stopped you at the tracks, told you
to listen to the rear and side mirrors (shiny as jack knives),
and thrown the gear shift in reverse. I would've, but I can't.

Nothing would stop you pummeling towards those train tracks,
a grin on your face and your belly fulla feel good juice.

If I could've gotten you to ignore your three buddies
egging you on, their non-stop *c'mon tom, you can beat it*
repeating in your head like a death march. If I could've told
you my cousins would sob nightly wondering what daredevil
robbed them of their father, I would've. Instead I will just pen
this poem, finish this glass of tart memories, and cringe every night
I hear freight car wheels screeching somewhere
far off in the distance.

Dear Dorothy/Diana
~A tribute to Michael Jackson

Dorothy, it was always about the Scarecrow. It was never about you
and your tired red shoes, clicking themselves into a wish, sparkling

into darkness. You whined about Auntie Em and Uncle Henry while he
wished for more between his cranium walls than spaghetti. You loved him then

as you do now. His fuzzy afro and yellow dandelion straw sticking out
of his pants like a dream. Even the child in me saw the whimsical way he gazed

at you, his brown fingers interlocked with yours. I loved watching you two ease
down those bricks, unstoppable, headed for the wizard. Skipping down

a road full of demise, a road full of promise, on a quest to be more
than shooting stars leaving your dust behind. And perhaps

the wizard didn't know, but you did Diana. You knew how fleeting
his star was. Even if he found his brains, his bright light was already

beginning to wane. Not you, the tin man, lion, or dancing trashcans could save
the scarecrow's delicate orb of light. He was always a constellation
speeding non-stop towards heaven.

Call Him Anything, but

a) The only time she saw the father happy was late Friday nights when he came home screeching Cutlass tires. Outside, he'd hum the Isleys slow, shuffle to the steps, scraping the metal key against the lock.

b) Once inside he'd sway towards the bed, wearing Old Grand-Dad like cologne, and strip down to boxer briefs. They were a white snowdrift against his hard brown skin. They hung off his body the same way a delicate doily barely covers a hard maple wood table top. The daughter's only job was to cover him, after he passed out, with Grandma's knitted blanket, the other woman who loved him too tight, while he looked up at her and smiled.

c) The first one all week.

d) She wants to call him liar, pretender, master of the night, man who wears Old Grand-Dad like cologne. The man she'll avoid in all her future boyfriends.

e) She wants to call him anything but daddy.

USA Roller Rink

You weren't American if you didn't go there as a pre-teen.
The only place in all of run-down South Bend, where
young people could all escape our own private hells:
the South East side projects, the wildness of the West
side, and the Midwestern factories closing their doors on all
our hungry mouths. Here we were reborn in the likeness
of Vaughan Mason & Crew. Their "Bounce, awwww SKATE" looped
in our ears as we brushed off our four wheels, used front stoppers
like tricycle training wheels we would never take off. Backwards,
frontwards, cross the leg over, we were indestructible bopping
to America's tune. Those who didn't skate would game in the corners,
jolt the joy stick, maneuvering Ms. Pac Man and conquering Centipede
with a swiftness. And sometimes old man Rufus, complete in shaggy overcoat,
would stand near the girl's bathroom, a stray right hand rambling
in his trousers, shifting from foot to foot until a cashier
would scold him away from the door. But none of this
mattered to us. The outer world in despair, and us inside working
our legs back and forth, making sure to get that perfect crossover,
dipping and diving over polished maple wood floors,
to whatever tune came over the speakers.

and Cornfields

Nestled between the Buckeyes and John Deere land sits the Hoosier State.
It is home to grassy knolls, home of Dillinger and Larry Bird, home of Axl Rose's
rock and roll, and America's King of Pop. Our dear Michael, a brilliant rosebud
born to an iron fist father. A similarity we share like twins. But Michael's music
was his lifejacket in a hostile home and out among a sea of doubtful blue eyes.
Indiana houses Bonnie Doon ice cream, boasting their perfectly blond mascot
on each package. And even after Obama's election, confederate flags still appear
way too often in my rear view mirror. It is home to Notre Dame, Dyngus Day
and pierogies, and beer-drinking partygoers dressed up in red and white.
They always party downtown, miles away from trailer parks which pepper flat
    landscape
like white polka dots on a black dress, the tenants standing shoeless
at the front doorstep, eyes spewing venom at brown skin. But most importantly,
Indiana is home of the surprise thunderstorm. Skies darken from azure blue
to steely grey, and the clouds huddle together over cornfields,
ready to momentarily bless green stalks with rain before moving out
in search of greener pastures.